598
Sha
c.1

Shackelford, Nina
Bird nests

Date Due

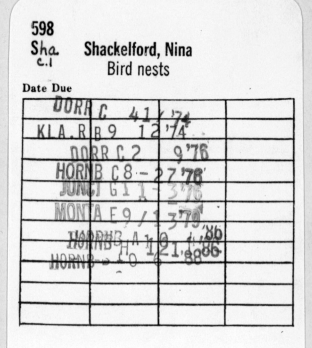

DORR C 41 '74		
KLA.R B 9 12 '74		
DORR C 2 9 '76		
HORNB C 8 - 27 '76		
JUN G 1 1 - 3 '79		
MONTA E 9 / 1 3 '79		
HORNB A 10 121 '86		
HORNB 10 4 88		

Nest construction shapes, sizes, materials, locations. How a robin builds his nest, in detail.

BIRD NESTS

B

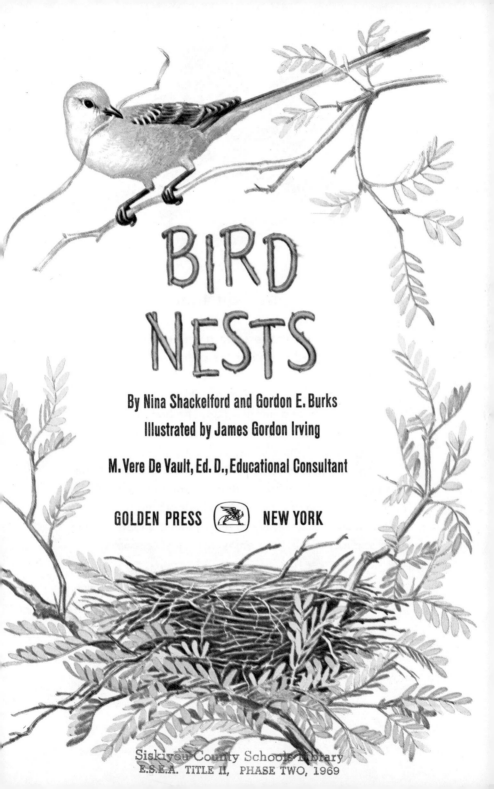

BIRD NESTS

By Nina Shackelford and Gordon E. Burks

Illustrated by James Gordon Irving

M. Vere De Vault, Ed. D., Educational Consultant

GOLDEN PRESS   NEW YORK

Introduction

Golden Science Readers are a series of easy-to-read books, designed to satisfy the child's natural curiosity about the world in which he lives.

Each book contains factual information, presented with simplicity and imagination. The text and the illustrations work together to bring the child both pleasure and greater comprehension of the subject.

Parents and teachers will welcome this additional source of self-help information for young readers. With the stimulation of these Golden Readers, boys and girls can grow in their ability to read, in their understanding of science, and in their enjoyment of good books.

M. Vere DeVault
Professor of Education,
University of Wisconsin

Library of Congress Catalogue Card Number: 62-12870

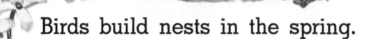

Birds build nests in the spring.

They build them for their eggs.

They build them for their young.

5

Birds build nests in many places.

Hawks build high in tree tops.

Pintails build on the ground.

Woodpeckers make nests in hollow trees.

Coots make nests on ponds.

Ospreys nest near the seacoast—

sometimes in trees,

or on cliffs,
or on the ground.

Bluebirds nest in birdhouses.

Swallows nest in barns.

These birds build no nests at all.

razor-billed auks

They lay their eggs on bare rock,
on cliffs beside the sea.

cowbirds

These birds build no nests of their own.

yellow warbler

They lay their eggs in other birds' nests.

11

Some sea birds nest in large colonies,
on islands along the coasts.

gannets

Grackles nest in small colonies,
in pine and cypress trees.

The nests of birds have many shapes.

The nest of the oriole looks like a bag hanging from a branch.

The nest of the swift looks like a dish, fixed to a chimney wall.

This dome-shaped nest is an ovenbird's nest.
The entrance is on the side.

What looks like a pile of sticks in a tree
is the nest of the great blue heron.

Some bird nests are very large.

The nest of the eagle
is as big as a bed. (7 feet across)
The eagle uses the same nest
year after year.
Every year, the eagle adds
more sticks and branches.
And so the nest keeps growing.

Some bird nests are very small.

The nest of the hummingbird,
the tiniest bird,
is about the size of a nut.
(1 inch across)

Although it is so small,
the nest holds not one,
but two tiny eggs.

Birds make nests of many things.

The cardinal uses roots and leaves.

The bittern uses reeds and grass.

Crows use twigs and sticks.

Plovers use sand and pebbles.

Ducks and geese
line their nests
with downy feathers
from their breasts.

eider

They pull them out with their bills
and make up downy beds.

long-eared owl

Owls use old nests that
other birds have given up.

great horned owl

Most birds take great care
in building their nests.
This is how robins
build their nests:
First they find a good place to build—

in the woods,

near a house,

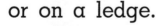

or on a ledge.

The male and female robin
build the nest together.
They bring twigs to the place
and put them in a circle
about the size of a cup.

The robins find hair
or bits of string,
and tie the twigs together.

They bring mud to the nest
with their bills
and fill up all the cracks.

Robins line their nest to make it soft.
For the lining they use grass, cotton,
feathers, rags, or soft bark.

The female shapes the lining to fit her body.
Then her work is done.

When a bird has built her nest,
she is ready to lay her eggs.
Some birds lay many eggs.
The bobwhite lays up to eighteen.

Other birds lay few eggs.
The pigeon lays two or three.

Some birds hatch their eggs quickly.
The sparrow hatches her eggs
in only twelve days.

Other birds hatch their eggs slowly.
The mallard takes four weeks.

Most parent birds feed their young
as long as they stay in the nest.
The parents fly back and forth
with worms, insects, berries, fish,
or whatever food they eat.

The young birds leave the nest
as soon as they are strong enough
to fly and hunt food for themselves.
And in the springs to come,
when they are fully grown,
they, too, will build nests
for their eggs and young.